Framing Techniques
& Decorating Ideas

AARON BROTHERS

Framing Techniques
& Decorating Ideas

AARON BROTHERS

Sterling Publishing Co., Inc. New York
A Sterling/Chapelle Book

Chapelle, Ltd.:
Jo Packham, Sara Toliver, Cindy Stoeckl

A Red Lips 4 Courage Book
Eileen Cannon Paulin, Rebecca Ittner,
Catherine Yarnovich Risling, Jayne Cosh

Red Lips 4 Courage Communications
8502 E. Chapman Ave., 303
Orange, CA 92869
(714) 289-0139
e-mail: rl4courage@redlips4courage.com
web site: www.redlips4courage.com

If you have any questions or comments, please contact:
Chapelle, Ltd., Inc., P.O. Box 9252, Ogden, UT 84409
(801) 621-2777 • (801) 621-2788 Fax
e-mail: chapelle@chapelleltd.com
web site: www.chapelleltd.com

Library of Congress Cataloging-in-Publication Data

Framing techniques & decorating ideas / Aaron Brothers.
   p. cm.
   "A Sterling/Chapelle Book."
   Includes bibliographical references and index.
   ISBN 1-4027-1485-8
   1. Picture frames and framing. 2. Decoration and ornament.
I. Aaron Brothers
(Firm) II. Title: Framing techniques and decorating ideas.
TT899.2.F73 2004
749'.7–dc22
                                        2004014764

10 9 8 7 6 5 4 3 2 1
Published by Sterling Publishing Co., Inc.
387 Park Avenue South, New York, NY 10016
©2004 by Aaron Brothers
Distributed in Canada by Sterling Publishing
c/o Manda Group, 165 Dufferin Street
Toronto, Ontario, Canada M6K 3H6
Distributed in Great Britain by Chrysalis Books Group PLC,
The Chrysalis Building,
Bramley Road, London W10 6SP, England
Distributed in Australia by Capricorn Link (Australia) Pty. Ltd.
P. O. Box 704, Windsor, NSW 2756, Australia
Printed and Bound in China
All Rights Reserved

Sterling ISBN 1-4027-1485-8

It seems no matter which magazine we open, or what home decorating show we may be watching, there's inevitably a focus on photographs.

Photographs are an indelible link to our past and heartwarming reminders of our present—the loves of our life and the friendships we hold near to our hearts; family vacations and weekend getaways with best friends; your kindergartener's first masterpiece or your baby's christening. Memories are captured not only in photographs, but also in the special mementos we take away on these very special days.

We choose photographs in both black and white and in color to line our shelves and adorn our walls. The beauty of photographs is that they look fantastic in every home, and depending on the frame chosen, they can even reflect a particular theme or décor.

Have you ever noticed the cohesive look of a montage of eclectic frames clustered together on an otherwise blank wall? This was not by chance. Choosing the right frames—and the images to fill them—is a science. Hanging them properly also requires some know-how and who better than the experts at Aaron Brothers to share their framing secrets?

One thing Aaron Brothers has learned is that frames are not just for snapshots. We frame artwork and poster prints; textiles and jewelry; documents and degrees. Life is art and it's meant to be framed. Just about anything can become a work of art.

Throughout this book we will explore the many ways to frame an object—from photographs to wedding cake toppers to silver medals. Since 1946, the folks at Aaron Brothers have been offering custom framing services.

Over the years they have learned just about everything there is to know about framing and are eager to share their expertise.

After all, photographs, artwork and collectibles reflect who we are, where we've been and the people who helped get us there. And what artwork could be more beautiful than these?

TABLE OF CONTENTS

(Above) The Aaron Brothers–Almore and Len–returned from military duty after World War II and founded a photography studio in Hollywood, California. After seeing their customers' needs for frames, they opened the first Aaron Brothers frame store.

(Opposite) When the store opened in 1946, it quickly became popular with show business personalities.

Framers to the Stars

The history of Aaron Brothers is as colorful as the artwork its frames have surrounded over the years. Founded in the early 1940s by two brothers as different as night and day, the company has long been an expert in framing techniques and styles. With more than 150 stores, Aaron Brothers plans to become the nationally recognized authority providing decorating ideas and solutions for art, framing, and displaying memorabilia.

Almore and Len Aaron joined the Armed Forces during World War II. One brother was stationed at Hal Roach Studios with Commanding Officer Ronald Reagan and the other brother took charge of a photo lab in Anchorage, Alaska. After their discharge from the service, they returned to Hollywood, California and opened a photography studio.

Noticing that most of their customers' photos ended up gathering dust in drawers, the brothers began selling photo frames. In 1946, Aaron Brothers opened its first frame shop in Hollywood. The store quickly attracted show business personalities and grew to include 16 more stores in the late 1950s and 1960s. As the "framer to the stars," Aaron Brothers' custom framing service was born.

Al and Len were determined that the business should be fun and adventurous. Art supplies were added in 1969, and by the 1970s, the stores were pioneers in mass marketing quality prints and paintings. As trends have come and gone, store inventory has included macramé, decoupage, batik, pottery and candle-making supplies.

Aaron Brothers became an institution with its "One Cent Frame Sale," which offers customers a second frame at one cent with the purchase of a frame of the same or greater value. The company has seen many frame fashions over the years, from the small sedate frames of the 1940s to the gaudy, rustic wood styles of the 1960s, to the popular pewter, bamboo and distressed frames of today.

(Above) Styles have come and gone (in this case, thank goodness!), yet the importance of framing is ever-growing as we amass more memories to frame, cherish and share.

(Opposite) Believing that the customers should enjoy the shopping experience, Aaron Brothers has been committed to as many choices in frames as there are tastes in style. During the late 1970s, shoppers were invited to "Honk for a Salesperson" whenever they needed assistance.

And while customers no longer toot a bicycle horn to summon help in the store, Aaron Brothers offers an array of products and services that span from small tabletop and photo frames to open wood frames for artwork, to services that include custom framing and matting for a variety of uses. Aaron Brothers has brought fashionable and affordable frames to the masses in addition to educating consumers about the best ways to display and preserve artwork and photographs. In this book, Aaron Brothers' framing and design experts share their expertise, as well as a variety of ideas and projects for making treasured objects and images a focal point in your home.

The Basics

There are countless frames available these days; it's a dizzying notion picking just one. If you are planning a wall arrangement, for example, you can go sophisticated (hand-carved gilded frames), simple and modern (clip or float frames), or somewhere in between.

If you're framing items other than fine art, photographs or posters, you'll likely need a deeper space to display your items. Or if it's a Renoir original, you'll undoubtedly be looking for an antique or custom frame with pre-servation in mind.

Not every frame comes in every size, but there are common measurements in the world of framing. Remember, if it's not a standard size or material, you'll be paying significantly more. Your choice will depend on the look you want, the price you can afford and the impact you desire. So before you go shopping, read on to learn about the variety of choices available.

(Opposite) Frames today are made for every style of home décor and can accommodate just about any sort of artwork.

Standard Frame Sizes

Wall frame standard sizes: 8"x10", 8½"x11", 11"x14", 16"x20" and 24"x36".

Other sizes include: 5"x7", 8"x12", 10"x13", 11"x17", 12"x36", 20"x28", 20"x30", 22"x28" and 27"x40".

Poster frame sizes: 24"x36" and 27"x41".

Frameology

Box Frame: Frameless style. Box frames are acrylic boxes with an insert that slides in to press the framed item to the front of the box.

Clip Frame: Frameless style. Clip frames have metal or plastic clips that hold the glass against the backing so that the item being "framed" is sandwiched between them. Glass is a polished or ground edged glass.

Closed-Corner Frame: Hand-carved or featuring elaborate ornamentation applied to the corners.

Custom Frame: Wood or metal moulding cut to desired size, and then assembled. Ornate styles are cut randomly at the corners on the diagonal so the pattern may not match at the corners.

Float Frame: Simple frame with artwork held between two pieces of glass. Wall behind is seen through the frame, thus wall color serves as the "mat."

Open Wood Frame: Ready-made frames in standard sizes that do not include the glass and backing. Usually have a fabric or self-liner and are intended for use with paintings on canvas or portraits.

Photo Frame: Also referred to as tabletop frames, smaller sizes with an easel back for display on a desk, mantel, etc.

Poster Frame: Simple and narrow frames, often plastic, that use a thin styrene sheet rather than glass. Frame is held together by an extruded plastic strip.

Scrapbook Frame: Square frame made to accommodate the pages of a scrapbook.

Shadowbox: Frames for dimensional objects with deep mouldings where the sides are lined with material to match the backing. Also referred to as keepsake box frames.

Wall Frame: Ready-made or keepsake frames in standard sizes for display on a wall.

CHAPTER 1

Framing Your Lifestyle

Everyone has a favorite photograph. More likely, every one of us has a box of favorite photographs. But when it comes to framing, we don't limit ourselves to these cherished snapshots. Limited-edition prints, oil paintings, watercolors, old letters, drawings, posters, diplomas and certificates adorn our walls. In our everyday lives we have found inspiration to create new types of artwork that incorporate historical events, fond memories, favorite things and even sports memorabilia.

Within our walls we take comfort in our memories—reminiscing with old friends, sharing vacation photos, savoring and showing off that one great shot. Our precious mementos are dear to our hearts and there's nothing that pleases us more than to artfully arrange them for all to see. What we choose to hang on our walls is a reflection of who we are.

We are no longer content with a basic frame or two; we cover our walls, line our shelves and choose furnishings that have a slot or two in which to slip in photos. Our tabletops have become a canvas for expressing our creativity, small spaces where we combine framed art, flowers and more for a spectacular still life that would make Van Gogh smile.

(Opposite) If your decorating style is country cottage, painted white and whitewashed frames are the ideal choice for your floral prints.

(Right) A collection of antique and vintage-style mirrors gives a bedroom a cozy, romantic style.

Our lifestyles are mirrored in the artwork we hang and the frames we choose. The more thoughtful of us contemplate which mat to use, or better yet, how many mats will showcase our artwork best. Size and proportion does matter when we're framing, so we need to consider our space and how to fill it well.

Thinking outside the box reveals an endless number of possibilities. Photographs and paintings typically come to mind when we think of frames, but don't forget about mirrors. Mirrors reflect the beauty of our surroundings and are a wonderful way to make small spaces appear larger. The power of the print can also be adopted in small spaces, where a large landscape with a faraway horizon creates the illusion of more space.

(Above) A well-lit piece of artwork takes center stage when hung in the right location and reflects the homeowner's personal style.

(Opposite) Mirror the sophisticated tone in your home with a regal gold frame for your oil paintings.

(Right) Dual images lend credence to the belief that two is better than one when it comes to visual impact.

There are frameless frames and nostalgic frames; frames with children's motifs and frames to hold vacation photos. We frame buttons and book pages, seashells and textiles. In a nutshell, we frame it all.

There are frames that are round, oval, square, horizontal and vertical. Wood frames can be painted, stained or left untreated. There are metal and faux metal frames and frames that are made to look aged. The resounding beauty of the frame is that we don't have to choose just one type. We can add a silver frame to an arrangement of gold frames, or combine metal frames with frames of painted wood. You may live in a 1920s cottage, but it's perfectly all right to incorporate contemporary frames. Your furniture may be antique but bright, white frames displayed with black-and-white photos will certainly update your décor.

(Above) Rather than one large piece of art above the bed, which could pose a safety risk if not hung correctly, a series of three smaller prints are just as appealing.

(Opposite) The items we choose to fill our homes—whether they're drawings, watercolors or prints—reflect refined tastes and affinity for a particular style.

The right frame doesn't overpower an image; it enhances its beauty and creates a dramatic effect. Big, ornate frames reflect the importance of an event; thin, simple frames reflect the subtleties of nature. Frames help tell a story and dress a room with intrigue.

Just as our rooms vary in color and character, so too can the artwork we choose to adorn our walls and reflect our spirit. There's little mystery in the things we treasure—it's revealed in their placement and presentation.

(Above) Snapshots from a favorite day at the ocean are right at home with a beach or tropical theme.

(Opposite) From the bed to the wall, framed textiles mirror their surroundings.

Personal Style

Frame styles reflect your personal taste. Here's what to look for:

Beach/Tropical: Bamboo and rattan styles, pickled pine or driftwood and whitewashed maple.

Contemporary: Slim, wide, beaded and brushed metal. Simple profiles with with little or no design in wood or metal. Satin, black or colored finishes. Metallic foils and simple leafed frames.

Formal: Elaborate silver or gold carved woods. Often incorporates a fabric liner.

French Country: White painted, embellished woods. Wire-brushed woods such as oak or pine.

Ornate: Many frames with composition ornamentation are in the style of carved period frames.

Rustic: Twig, untreated or recycled wood.

Traditional: Furniture-finish wood tones and gold or silver leafed styles with a simple design element.

Vintage: Black or brown ovals. Can also be white, gold or silver.

CHAPTER 2

Wall Arrangements

Nothing is more befitting a blank wall than an arrangement of framed images. The beauty in the mixing and matching is that black fits well with pewter, and white is just as complementary with either one. You can choose wood or metal, or a combination of both. Some of the most intriguing arrangements are thinking-out-of-the-box configurations that turn a plain space into an extraordinary place.

Different colors of frames can make a striking statement when combined in a wall grouping. Black and brown used together, for example, can create a sophisticated, urban look. A grouping of all-white painted frames would certainly suggest French Country decor. When using two or more frame colors it's important to keep the frames and matting the same style to establish a unified, planned look and avoid an overly busy wall.

You can choose a simple three-in-a-row pattern of like frames with different images in the same theme or family of hues; or cover an entire staircase wall with images of smiling children, wedded couples and memorable family snapshots.

If this sounds like too much or too little, somewhere in between you can find the right combination for any space. It may be difficult at first, but with a little guidance and inspiration from the photographs and ideas that fill the pages of this book, you'll be able to put together the look you desire.

(Opposite) When framing artwork that is distinctively different, select like frames to obtain a cohesive look.

(Right) Three in a row is a safe rule to follow when hanging a series of framed art. By choosing similar matting and frames, the artwork has uniform appeal.

(Above) Artwork, frames, furnishings and accessories pay tribute to the humble beginnings of our country.

(Opposite) When selecting a frame, consider the artwork. Here, Americana-themed prints are right at home with rustic wood frames.

Wall Cover

Whether you choose gold-leaf frames or an assortment of painted wood frames, the impact of an arrangement of frames is a striking way to show off your favorite paintings, treasured photos or pencil drawings. For a very symmetrical, uniform look, consider a series of wood frames hung right next to, and on top of, each other. Thin black frames with the same matting are an appealing combination for this clean look. If you're interested in a more formal look, gold-leaf or pewter frames in varying styles can pull together your different pieces of artwork. Don't be afraid to add a walnut frame with gold or silver accents to your wall arrangement. The question you need to answer is: Do you want to mix or do you want to match?

Collectors' Arrangement

Perhaps you collect album covers from the Jazz Age, Big Band era or the '60s, or vintage posters or signs with a patriotic flair. These items can make wonderful works of art and set a theme in a room. When it comes to choosing frames, be sure your choices enhance, rather than overshadow, the items to be framed. If your décor is primitive, consider twig frames or frames made from weathered or untreated wood. If your space is decorated in French Country, all-white frames are a good choice. And if the collection you are framing is vintage, you may want to choose a style reminiscent of the era of your collectibles. From handkerchiefs to postcards to magazine covers, there is little you cannot frame.

Mix It Up

Go one step further with your wall arrangement by introducing a few elements such as oversized wooden letters or vintage platters. A kitchen nook takes on a farmhouse feel with a vintage sign, framed prints and other themed elements on nearby tabletops. Majolica plates in a nearly all-white formal living room dress up adjacent prints with color and bring an interesting element to the room. Don't forget those fabulously framed mirrors— they're sure to open up the space. The more creative you are, the freer you'll feel to mix things up.

(Above) When choosing your artwork, stick to a common color found within all of the objects you plan to hang. In this case, blue was the hue of choice.

(Opposite) Wall art is no longer relegated to framed prints. Integrating collections, especially platters, plates and dishes, is a wonderful way to add dimension and color to a wall space.

Storytelling Arrangement

A close grouping of like frames can tell a story beautifully. Line up photos in chronological order; this way, you can preserve memories of a special event and witness life's natural progression. If you have a thin vertical space of wall to work with, consider four rows of two side-by-side frames. Perhaps you have a long side table with ample space above for a horizontal arrangement. Here, lining up horizontal frames in two rows of four frames side by side would create an impact. If you choose a grouping effect, keep your frames simple and position them close to each other. Remember, wider mats help set off the composition.

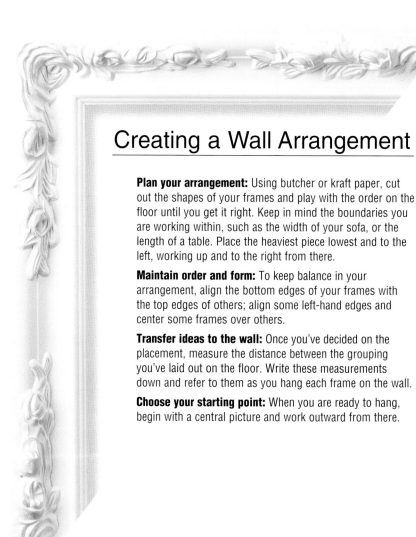

Creating a Wall Arrangement

Plan your arrangement: Using butcher or kraft paper, cut out the shapes of your frames and play with the order on the floor until you get it right. Keep in mind the boundaries you are working within, such as the width of your sofa, or the length of a table. Place the heaviest piece lowest and to the left, working up and to the right from there.

Maintain order and form: To keep balance in your arrangement, align the bottom edges of your frames with the top edges of others; align some left-hand edges and center some frames over others.

Transfer ideas to the wall: Once you've decided on the placement, measure the distance between the grouping you've laid out on the floor. Write these measurements down and refer to them as you hang each frame on the wall.

Choose your starting point: When you are ready to hang, begin with a central picture and work outward from there.

(Left) Lining up artwork in chronological order helps to tell your family story.

(Opposite) Selecting unexpected placement for your wall arrangement can only enhance the images—and lend visual impact to the room.

Shelves And Mantels

Mantels are often a favorite place to adorn with seasonal elements, and their positioning as a focal point means they offer countless decorating opportunities. You can hang a framed mirror above the mantel along with a series of photographs or simply lean an ornate mirror and smaller photo against the wall, then add other items such as candles or a vase of fresh flowers. Here is a wonderful location to show off a sophisticated piece of art or series of framed elements.

Layer Upon Layer

Layering picture frames, meaning, a smaller print that rests in front of a larger framed print or two, is a contemporary approach to décor. This technique can be used on mantels, shelves, desks and tables. Some hints to layering:

Size: Variation of size is very important for contrast. Larger pieces are usually behind smaller ones.

Amount: An odd number of pieces creates a more eye-catching presentation.

Unity: Make sure there is an element that ties all the frames together—frame moulding, color, texture or images.

(Opposite) Combining a wall arrangement with mantel décor is a striking way to bring impact to a room.

(Below) Layering frames is a unique option for mantels and shelves.

Creating Shelf Space

If you find that you can leave no shelf bare, and you've just about run out of space for figurines and frames, there's no need to worry. A wall shelf—or series of shelves—provides an easy solution to creating more shelf space. Wall shelves give depth to your photo arrangement and make a particular space more interesting. You can illuminate the space with ambient lighting, spotlighting the images below, or you can simply use natural light to make your photos stand out.

(Above and below) If you've run out of room, an easy-to-hang wall shelf provides extra display space.

(Opposite) Wall shelves come in a variety of sizes and when more than one is used, they beautifully fill in an otherwise blank space. Just be sure to plan for enough room between the shelves to give your artwork space.

Small Budget Gallery

Money need not be an obstacle to creating a pleasing wall arrangement. Simple acrylic box frames can be arranged in symmetrical rows to display a favorite set of prints or book pages. The pages of a favorite calendar, maps, small posters, greeting cards and magazine pages are good choices for inexpensive art displays. With a little imagination the options are endless, and you can afford to change the display as often as you wish.

(Above) From calendar pages to large stationery prints, artwork can be housed in simple acrylic box frames.

(Left) Pages from a book become storytelling artwork for a child's room.

(Opposite) Acrylic rather than glass is a safe alternative to glass frames, especially when hung in children's rooms.

Keeping Things Straight

To hang a row of pictures, begin by stretching two pieces of string between pushpins to represent the top and bottom edges of the frames. Use a level gauge to make sure the strings are straight. For the bottom of the frames, measure the distance from the top of the frame to the mid point of the hanging wire pulled taut. Make the distance from the string to the bottom of the picture hook the same. Repeat the process if you are hanging more than one row of frames.

(Above) When hanging a series of items, experts recommend keeping your center focus eye level.

(Opposite) The wall serves as the matting for these float frames containing handkerchiefs. Remember to leave the same amount of space between each frame edge.

CHAPTER 3

Memory Boxes

A picture may be worth a thousand words, but the small trinkets and baubles we cherish can tell a story of great love, a historical period in time or a fairy-tale wedding. We create memories every single day; some are more sentimental than others and inspire us to collect mementos that mark that special day, event or person.

How many drawers in your home are filled with old baby spoons and cups, or shoeboxes stuffed with maps, rail tickets and postcards from that trip of a lifetime? What compels us to stash away these items, or grow our collections large and small, should also lead us down the frame store aisle to shadowboxes.

Shadowboxes are a wonderful way to display and preserve family heirlooms, sports memorabilia or treasured collectibles. They add a unique element to rooms, regardless of décor, and share a wonderful story or passion. The depth of these shadowboxes, also referred to as object box frames, is typically one or two inches, but shadowboxes can be custom made to fit just about any desired object. The frame can be small enough to hold a winning golf ball, or large enough in which to hang a collection of cherished family memorabilia. With this flexibility in space, the types of items that can be framed are endless.

(Opposite) An old letter, calligraphy pen and framed photos tell a story of long-gone but not forgotten relatives.

(Right) By having your mat board custom cut, a shadowbox can accommodate just about any size photo or piece of memorabilia.

Links To The Past

There is something very intriguing about old things—hand-tinted photographs dating back to the 1880s; your mother's favorite chintz teacup and saucer; a tarnished silver stopwatch; storied war medals, their ribbons nearly faded. Some of these items can be linked to a great-great grandfather you never knew, or an uncle whose long-unused pipe still smells of cherry tobacco. Perhaps you just love to collect old things, imagining the woman whose love letter had somehow been saved and fatefully ended up in your hands, or whose beaded purse had been witness to the bustling events in a grand ballroom or two. A shadowbox allows you to share a story by combining nostalgic elements with a three-dimensional effect.

(Above and left) Vintage family treasures can inspire a framed box of memorabilia.

(Opposite) Rather than relegate cherished silver baby utensils to a drawer, identify each piece and mount in a silver-frame shadowbox.

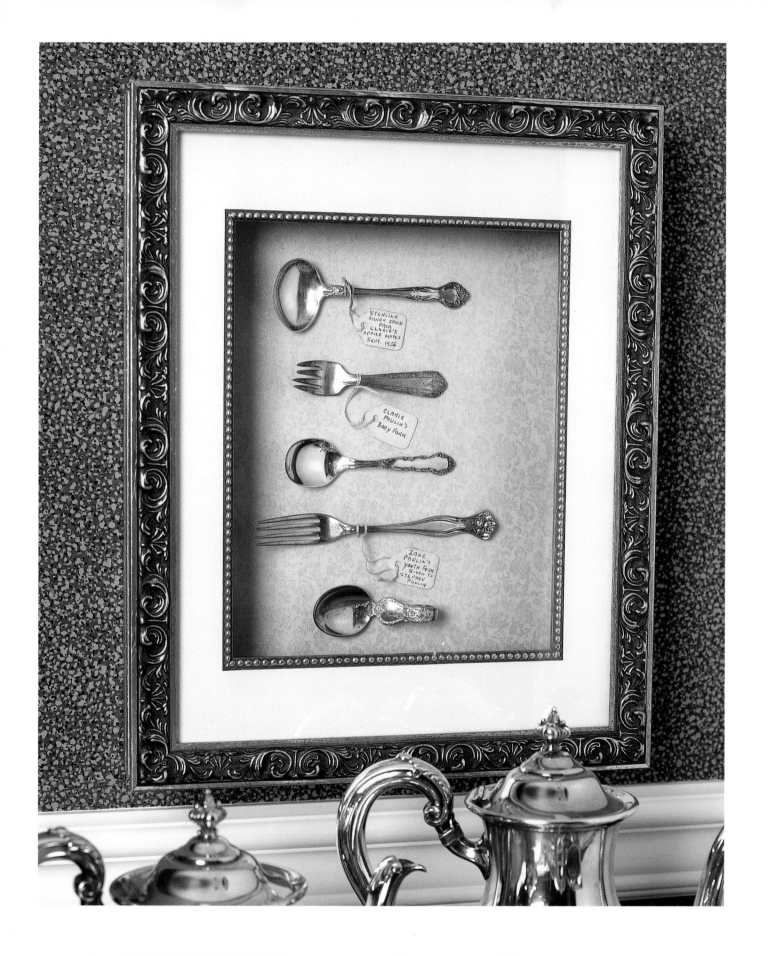

Planes, Trains & Automobiles

If you have a handful of ticket stubs from the Metro in Paris or the Underground in London, you're a collector. The same is true if you've kept the hotel and restaurant receipts, sky diving brochure and local currency you picked up while honeymooning in Tahiti. These things may have little or no monetary value, but their intrinsic value is priceless. They can evoke smiles, or even tears, and parting with them has somehow become unthinkable. Whether it's a small assortment of items, or a series of the same item, such as seashells or wine labels, travel souvenirs can be artfully arranged in a shadowbox that fits in just about any décor.

(Above and opposite) Mementos such as photographs, train tickets, maps, and even items indigenous to a particular part of the world are the makings for a storytelling travel collage.

Attaching Your Collectibles

Under a mat: This technique is referred to in the trade as "sink mount." When displaying items behind a mat opening, you can add strips of foam board or mat board to "shim up" the back to support the item on all sides. Good for combining photographs or documents and dimensional items. *Ideal for:* ceramic tiles, sand paintings, icons.

Sew to backing: A simple loop stitch around the object can secure it to the box. Use a thread type similar to the fabric being secured; for non-textile objects, use cotton-covered polyester. Do not use fishing line, as it stretches over time and can damage delicate textiles. *Ideal for:* jerseys, christening gowns, cake-cutting utensils, baby books, silk fans.

Recess in backing: Cut an opening slightly smaller than the dimension of the object, then rest object in the "well." Good option for fairly heavy items. *Ideal for:* baseballs, baseball bat, child's plaster handprint cast, golf ball collection.

Attach with clips: Small acrylic clips available at frame stores attach to the back of the box with a small post and retaining collar. Good option for thin items that cannot be stitched. *Ideal for:* coins, plates, spoons, ceramic tiles, sand paintings, decorative plaques.

Secure with moulding: Sections or corners of moulding can be used to fabricate a shelf on which to rest object (object needs to be attached to shelf to prevent shifting). Good option for thick items. *Ideal for:* teacups, porcelain figurines, wedding cake toppers.

Affix with adhesive: Silicone adhesive provides a flexible bond that can be peeled from a smooth surface for easy removal. Hot glue is another option, however, it does not hold as securely as silicone. Use only as a last resort; adhesive and valuable, irreplaceable or sentimental items don't mix. *Ideal for:* metal and glazed ceramics.

Scrapbook Frames

With all of the dynamic scrapbooking embellishments and techniques available, some layouts look like they're right out of an artist's studio. Square frames especially designed to hold these pages preserve the work of creative minds in style. These frames are deeper than a standard picture frame to accommodate the pages, and make a striking accompaniment to a shadowbox, and to preserve and showcase larger items.

(Above and opposite) Scrapbooking has become a favorite pastime and with frames made specifically for these compilations, creative pages become works of art worth hanging.

CHAPTER 4

Photo Frame Vignettes

While wall frames preserve photographs and display artwork out of reach at eye level, photo frames are their little cousins ideal for everyday snapshots. As they are fitted with an easel backing, these frames are perfect for dressing up coffee tables, consoles, end tables and desks. Embellishments have made frames themselves works of art; you can find frames with crystals, pearls, painted flowers and embroidered silk. You'll find frames with cutouts such as celestial forms or beautifully adorned with words such as "Mother," "Family" and "Friends."

The variety of photo frames available invite us to express our creativity and share our stories of good times and favorite sentiments. Items such as a trio of candles and a vase of fresh-cut flowers are paired with framed photographs to create a table scape right out of a magazine. And it's not just decorators and designers who have clued in to the impact of vignettes, or, small groupings of accessories; everyone seems to be getting out their memorable items to set next to a photograph. What could be better suited next to a

photograph of you and your family playing in the roaring waves of the Pacific Ocean than a handful of shells and a jar of sand collected on a favorite vacation? Or, remember a favorite auntie by displaying her photo along with her silver vanity set and pearls.

(Opposite) Ornate frames such as these etched-glass ones are best paired with simple black-and-white photographs.

(Right) A vignette can be created in an unconventional spot such as the frame of an iron daybed.

(Above) Vignettes are ideal storytellers that allow us to pair images with trinkets from a favorite period in time, like a vacation at the beach.

(Opposite) When lining a space with assorted frames, be sure to vary their heights, even if it means stacking books for height.

Finding Space

If you've run out of tabletop space, consider a window ledge, plate rack, atop an armoire or simply add a row or two of moulding to craft your magic. An iron étagère lined with plants, framed photos and a stack or two of books becomes an interesting piece indoors. Imagine the impact of a collection of Creamware pitchers interspersed with black-and-white photos in thin black frames! The vintage theme also can be achieved when black-and-white photos in simple oval, square and rectangular frames are placed together. Just remember to vary your heights of frames, or place some of the frames on makeshift pedestals, such as old books.

A quick look around your home will surely turn up the perfect mix of shapes and textures to accompany photographs. Incorporate personal mementos, interesting objects from travels, handed-down accessories or found items from flea markets or antique haunts. There's a vignette for every décor; basic black frames with bamboo shoots in a clear glass vase suggest a Zen-inspired space, while white-painted frames next to a bountiful arrangement of lavender is not only fragrant, it speaks of a country-inspired decor.

Each room offers dozens of decorating possibilities. Consider the room and the space that will be filled. The height and placement of objects will dictate their balance. You can choose one frame or a multiple of frames. You should, however, select from the same family of frames—all wood or all metal—or the same color, for a cohesive look.

Great Groupings

When designing a tabletop display, keep in mind the following:

- Create a "landscape" vignette by varying the shapes and sizes of the frames and accompanying objects.
- Use books as risers to elevate frames and/or accessories.
- Group together framed photos that share a style, such as all contemporary frames or all vintage-style frames.
- Remember that highly embellished frames look better with black-and-white photographs.

Living Room

Create a sophisticated, traditional feel by combining an elaborate silver frame with a glimmering candelabrum and silver bowl of wooden spheres. Celebrate a particular season with theme-related accessories. During October, for example, display a photo of your son in a pumpkin patch next to cornhusks, gourds and pumpkins for a three-dimensional effect. Throughout the month of December, a photograph in a pewter frame from the previous Christmas would look stunning atop your mantel with a trio of silver candlesticks and a container of ornaments.

(Right) This gold antiqued frame looks very rich against the dark wood furniture.

(Opposite) A commonality is achieved with three different frames in the same color, unifying different images.

Quiet Retreat

Every tabletop is a blank canvas. Create a picture-perfect setting with a treasured photograph of your mother, old glass perfume bottles and a vintage brush and comb set on your vanity. Or, consider a vanity tray topped with three gold-leaf frames of varying heights and styles for a uniform look. The addition of a silver pitcher or vase would fill in a larger space well. If your bedroom is a large master suite consider putting small square tables on either side of the bed. Use the table on your side of the bed to display your family pictures and memorabilia and on your husband's side display his family photographs and favorite keepsakes. You can add a soothing lavender candle and two lamps with three-way light bulbs so that each of you can relax or read, whichever is your preference.

(Right) Some of the best matches for a lone display frame is a vase of flowers and a lighting fixture.

(Opposite) Whether it's a bedside table or a desk next to the bed, just about any tabletop beckons assorted frames and accessories.

Kitchen

If you have a shelf to spare, consider hanging a framed print or two of fruit, then lining up a few faux pieces of fruit on the shelf below. Vintage kitchen utensils, collectible tin canisters or enamel teapots would work well too. If your shelf space is limited, the top of your cabinets or a single piece of storage furniture is befitting a tabletop display. A framed snapshot from a vacation to Provence would look spectacular next to a pot of herbs, a basket of fruit and a bottle of wine for a grouping that is both beautiful and functional.

They Go Together

Items that go well with tabletop photo arrangements:

- Urn
- Mantel clock
- Old hardcover books
- Candlesticks
- Vase of flowers
- Plants
- Decorative lamp
- Bowl of fruit
- Porcelain figurines
- Collectible china, glass
- Ceramic
- Swag of fabric

(Opposite) An elegant still life that incorporates food reflects the purpose of the kitchen.

Den/Family Rooms

There's no better place to show off a collection of old cameras or treasured calligraphy pens and inkwells than in your den or family room. Continue the vintage-inspired look with photographs in an assortment of frames. Break up a series of boring bookshelves with color photos in masculine pewter or leather frames, or for a woman's touch, frames in an assortment of colors.

(Opposite) Frames in graduating sizes, all in silver tones, make an attractive tablescape.

(Below) When you've run out of ideas for displaying treasured postcards from a seaside escape, consider a series of frames with natural textures and a bowl of shells.

(Above) Matting is not only the finishing touch; it protects and preserves the contents within a frame.

CHAPTER 5

Matting

Just as important as the frame you choose is the mat that accompanies it. A mat is the decorative border that surrounds the art. It is made from a special type of paperboard with an opening cut—generally with a bevel edge —for viewing the artwork. A mat has both decorative and mechanical functions, and is very important for valuable artwork and irreplaceable photographs. The purpose of the mat is to provide a visual separation between the art and the frame.

It is very important to keep in mind the colors of the artwork and the subject matter. For example, a textured rice paper mat is an interesting choice for a tropical print. Combine these two with a bamboo frame and you've got a cohesive look with the feel of the tropics.

You wouldn't dream of framing a Picasso in a plain metal frame without a mat. Likewise, a black-and-white retro poster framed with a black suede mat would certainly make a stunning statement. The mat you choose—whether it is suede, fabric or textural paper—is the finishing touch to lending a dramatic impact to your piece of art.

There are single, double and triple mats, and mats with wood, gold or silver fillets (a thin moulding used as an accent inside another moulding or at the edge of a mat opening window). There are embossed mats, and mats with various textures such as suede, chenille and grass cloth. Mat openings can be rectangular, square, oval, circular or arched. As you can see, the options in mat selection are numerous.

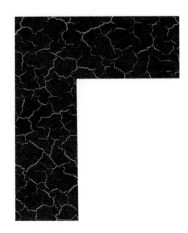

Mat Options

Besides the frame, the best way to enhance the impact of your artwork is through the choice of mat. Some things to consider:

Single mat: A single mat by itself can look two-dimensional and uninteresting. If the artwork requires the simplicity of a single mat color, consider adding dimension with a double-thick or eight-ply mat board, raised mats, decorative line cuts or even adding a second mat of the same color.

Double mat: A double mat is probably the most common approach to matting because it is simple to design, versatile and allows you to incorporate more intense color in the design without overpowering the work. Often, the top mat is a neutral color, while the bottom mat highlights a focal color in the art or matches the frame color.

Three or more mats: By adding more mat layers, you are able to build complex color harmonies and add nuances to the mat design. A multiple selection also helps bridge the transition from the art to the home decor, since you can work with colors from both the art and the space in which it will hang. When using more than two mats, vary the exposure of each layer.

Fillets: A fillet provides contrast between the art and matting. It is often selected to match the frame finish, which helps unify the framing design and draws the viewer's eye to the image. Fillets look especially attractive when combined with a fabric-covered mat. When a fillet is used with matting, the bevel is usually cut reversed so that the fillet is flush against the mat opening.

Wide mats: Extremely wide mats can lend a sense of importance and help to keep a piece from being overpowered by a frame with a strong design. A wide mat becomes especially important when using wider moulding. As a rule of thumb, the matting should be at least twice the width of the frame moulding.

Weighted or elongated mats: "Weighting" the mat (making the bottom mat border wider than the other three borders) provides a gallery look. Be sure to maintain proportion when the mat opening is extended down to accommodate a signature border on a signed and numbered print, or a title cut or plaque. Elongated mats (two opposing borders are wider than the other two borders) can be used to enhance the appearance of length or height.

(Opposite) The black-and-white details of simple mats create a sophisticated showplace for vintage photos.

Matting Guidelines

Mats can give a reproduction the stately effect of an original, and can make a diminutive piece of art seem awesome as the mat draws the viewer's eye into the picture without competing with the art. The solid color of a mat allows you to coordinate the colors of your room with your artwork, providing a "frame-within-a-frame" effect that sets off your piece. When arranging a cluster of different photographs, choosing the same color and style of mat is the key to a unified result and avoiding a hodge-podge of mismatched artwork. Opting for similar mats also prevents a wall from becoming too busy when hanging different frames.

If you're framing something with uneven edges—a piece of textile, for example—a mat gives the piece a nice, clean edge. A mat is also the ideal way to create a larger piece of artwork that makes a dramatic statement on an otherwise plain wall.

In addition to the aesthetic qualities, mats are essential in preserving artwork. While an 8"x10" photo may fit perfectly in a frame of the same size, moisture can condense over time inside the glass and cause damage to the image. The artwork, and especially photographs, can become stuck to the glass, making its removal impossible. A mat provides enough space between the image and the glass to keep the artwork intact. The mat also stabilizes the artwork, prevents bending and folding and conceals the mounting support mechanism.

While mats are available in a variety of materials including paper, cardboard and fibrous materials, higher quality mats are available in archival-quality material. Remember, the best choice in preserving artwork is an acid-free and lignin-free cotton or pure alpha cellulose mat, which also is fade-resistant and does not discolor.

Pre-Cut Mats

There are rows of pre-cut mats available at your local frame stores. Most mats range in width from 1 1/4" for smaller items, to 5" for prints that are 22"x30" or larger. You can buy single mats to fit standard-size frames, or you may want to consider more elaborate mats. Double mats provide a nice contrast, and some mats even feature creatively cut corners. There are pre-made mats for family collages, accommodating a dozen or so photographs, or you can find a mat with two picture openings to show off your twins.

Custom Mats

Just as frames come in various shapes, colors and sizes, so do mats. If you don't find the look you want among the selection of pre-made mats, you may want to consider the scores of cut-to-fit options. You can have a mat custom cut to frame a vinyl record and album cover, or a mat with a series of openings to tell a story in succession. Not only can you choose the material you want, you can choose the exact width of the mat, the way it is cut and even incorporate elements such as hearts or words into the custom cut.

Decorative Cut Mats

Used to echo the theme of the artwork, decorative cuts can be made at the corners. For example, a "v-groove" cut adds a thin border outside the mat opening, and complements art with strong linear elements; a step corner is right at home with Southwestern art or architectural prints; and rounded corners look great with Art Deco pieces and some Asian images.

Fabric Mats

Sometimes an image calls for a specific mat and frame. A wedding portrait is worthy of a cream or white silk background, while a row of antique buttons is perfectly suited to a beautiful vintage fabric. Don't be afraid to layer your fabrics or combine textiles and paper mats for a unique impact. Allowing your artwork to "float" on fabric provides the look of a mat, without the window effect. If you're framing a child's artwork, retain the charm of childhood by showing off the tattered edges—just layer the artwork atop fabric such as gingham. For an even more personal approach, consider embellishing your mats with ribbons, pearls, stencils or even sentimental words or thoughts written in calligraphy.

(Above) Matting turns a simple print into a piece of art.

(Opposite) A sleek, modern approach to framing black-and-white photographs is achieved by choosing the same frames and mats.

CHAPTER 6

Making It Your Own

Defining your style is an exciting progression, and often we can't find just the right option to suit our look. We thumb through scores of magazines, in search of the perfect wall color or the right combination of furniture. We are interested in how other people live and what they have in their homes. This curiosity leads us to develop our own signature style, unique to us and the things we surround ourselves with.

While there are countless frames available to suit just about every palette, there are some who prefer to personalize. You don't have to be an artist to take a very basic frame and create a decorative frame that is as sentimental as the photo it contains.

These simple frames are available in glass and acrylic, and are very inexpensive alternatives to typical photo frames. Or, you can choose a wooden frame with a smooth surface. Photo frames that are at least two inches wide work best.

Before you begin any project, consider the following: Which room is the frame for? What are the colors in that room? What is the theme? These answers will help you decide which look is best, and what colors you should choose. You may want to also consider the colors in the photograph you will be framing.

In addition to photo frames, you can fashion a custom look for a memo board with decorative elements such as buttons, ribbon, paint and more. The prime directive is to take a particular object from plain to pretty. Consider the following suggestions, or incorporating two or three, for a dazzling—and decidedly you—effect.

(Opposite and right) Simple embellishments such as buttons and beautiful ribbon transform a basic wooden box frame. All you need is a glue gun and some interesting touches like colorful or elaborate buttons.

Embellishments

There are so many wonderful elements that can be incorporated onto a frame to add dimension and interest. If you have a box of small seashells, create the ideal frame for a vacation photo by covering a plain wood frame with the shells. Buttons can be used in the same way, or as accents in the corners or lined up along the bottom of the frame. You may want to paint the frame first before adding buttons or other small elements such as beads or rhinestones. Tiny baubles can be used to create a fillet around the frame's opening or lined up to create a subtle harlequin pattern. Trophy shops also can engrave small metal plaques with a special message or distinction, which can be attached to a frame or mat.

(Above) What better way to frame a vintage photograph than to embellish the frame with antique buttons.

(Opposite) A fun way to create a new look for an old frame that also adds interest is adhering shells that can either be purchased at a crafts store or found on shoreline walks.

Paint

Just as paint can transform a room, paint has the power to change the look of a wood frame. Take a simple paint makeover one step further and stencil a favorite motif, such as leaves or flowers, or a short phrase or word such as "Love" or "Family." Age an outdated gold frame by lightly applying black paint, then quickly wiping it off to reveal slight traces of the paint. Stain can be used as a masculine alternative to paint. All you have to do is mark off sections of a wood frame with masking tape to create the desired result, whether it be striped, checkered or another pattern of your choice.

Paper

The simplicity of a clip frame or box frame can be dressed up with a unique approach to matting your artwork. Wallpaper, handmade textured paper, tissue paper and decoupage are all paper choices that can give an old mat a new look, while at the same time make over the frame. These paper choices can also be used to cover the frame itself.

(Opposite) Jewels are everywhere—inside, outside and even above this plain Jane frame-turned-aristocratic display.

(Above) Velvet milliner's flowers and leaves can be adhered to a simple painted frame to make it elegant.

Fabric

If you have an old frame that's chipped beyond repair, or has just lost its luster, you may want to cover it with fabric. If you prefer a patterned textile, remember to choose one with a small print or thin stripes. The fabric can be glued directly onto the surface; be sure to smooth out any bubbles. Or, incorporate some cotton filler for a different effect. This is a great idea if you want to match drapery, bedding or a lampshade. Ribbon and velvet roses are wonderful fabric embellishments either used alone or with fabric.

Quick Change

A frame does not necessarily have to surround a picture or a mirror. It can make an elegant showcase for a bulletin or memo board. Take some time to peruse the wood frame section in your local framing store. Generally, these are the frames made for canvases and other large artworks. Purchase an artist's canvas to fit the inside opening of the frame. Next, cover the frame with fabric. You may want to add a layer of batting between the canvas and the fabric for a soft look. Next, affix ribbons to the back of the canvas in a diagonal pattern crossing each other. Use picture mounts to attach the canvas to the frame.

Many collectors are buying pictures not for the artwork, but for their elaborate frames. Give an old frame new life by turning it into a mirror or memo board. Just be sure to carefully remove the artwork if you plan to keep it.

(Above) Fabric, a staple gun, picture mounts, tacks and an artist's canvas are all that's needed to create a memo board.

(Opposite and below) Ribbons hold photos and other memorabilia in place without the damage that pushpins can cause.

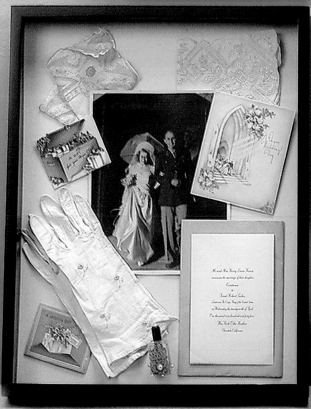

CHAPTER 7

Documents & Historical Memorabilia

From the moment we are born, a paper trail begins. A birth certificate denotes our arrival and vital statistics, which is followed some years later by a high school diploma and, for those who continue their education, a university degree—or two. To college graduates, a bachelor's, master's or doctorate degree represents several grueling years of hard work and the proof is in a certificate that sometimes never sees the light of day after graduation. Its value, nevertheless, is priceless.

Important documents encompass so much more than academic degrees and birth certificates. We are surrounded by historical mementos, and at the same time, we're accumulating papers that we tuck away in drawers and cabinets. Whether these documents are of interest only to us, our families, an entire town or a greater audience, it is important to take proper care to prevent their demise. Documents also can serve as sentimental reminders of our accomplishments and our heritage when they're framed and put on display. By choosing to frame such items, we also are choosing to preserve a personal legacy.

(Opposite) Paper items such as a wedding invitation, a baseball ticket or military documents inspire memorable displays.

(Right) Old, treasured letters are family documents and can be preserved in a framed display.

73

Endless Options

Letters, military release papers, news-papers and old certificates, and fabric or needlework are often found many years after being rolled up or folded. If they're really old, they've likely become tattered and torn. Before attempting to frame a brittle document, moisture needs to be restored to it. Remember, valuable documents cannot be replaced so you may want to consult a preservation expert.

Ready-made frames are frequently used for documents for their simplicity and afford-ability, but if you want to ensure a longer life, consider a custom frame with a more protective glass and a higher-grade mat. Laminating or mounting a document with adhesive are permanent techniques not recommended; they could potentially damage or lead to the deterioration of a document or greatly affect its value.

Framing documents along with a photograph or other mementos is a wonderful way to share a story. A marriage certificate, for example, is a natural companion to a photograph of the newly joined couple and perhaps their wedding invitation. Remember, a custom mat will graciously accommodate such a trio. And a Civil War document is the perfect fit among a wall arrangement of vintage samplers from the same era.

There's no need to limit your ideas to documents and certificates; history is all around us, telling of the past, and defining our future.

Center Stage

Give your piece the attention it deserves. Some elements to consider:

Choose an elaborate frame. A gilded or silver frame with a wide moulding will give the document a custom look.

Customize a quality mat. A suede, embroidered or richly textured mat takes an extraordinary approach to framing.

Add a fillet. Fillets are decorative elements that enhance the overall presentation and can complement and mirror the choice of frame.

Attach a pocket. An envelope at the back of the frame is a great place to keep materials related to the framed item.

(Opposite) Antique needlework speaks volumes about the times and people of long ago and lend a warm, nostalgic touch in our homes.

Matting A Document

Always use an archival mat with at least two layers when framing a document to provide enough air space to prevent condensed moisture from damaging the paper. Over time, ultraviolet light can discolor paper and render it brittle, as well as fade the printing. Use UV-filtering glass or acrylic to help slow the deterioration of a document.

Be sure to use archival photo corners to hold the document in place behind the mat. Stay away from pressure-sensitive tape, it can be damaging over time. Don't moisten or stretch a natural parchment before framing.

When matting, be sure to leave a little room for the paper to expand with humidity changes. Don't push the corners of the frame tightly against the edges of the document.

(Above) The last letter of a beloved grandfather is witness to the bond he shared with his granddaughter, especially when paired with family photos.

(Opposite) This real sheepskin diploma had been stored rolled up with some family belongings. It required a restoration expert and is now preserved in this dimensional frame.

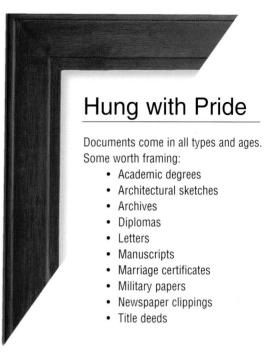

Hung with Pride

Documents come in all types and ages.
Some worth framing:

- Academic degrees
- Architectural sketches
- Archives
- Diplomas
- Letters
- Manuscripts
- Marriage certificates
- Military papers
- Newspaper clippings
- Title deeds

(Above) Masculine ready-made certificate frames display top honors in style and are an inexpensive way to show off achievements.

(Opposite) Custom framing enhances professional documents and looks excellent when hung in any office. Soften the look of an office by adding other collectibles, such as a needlepoint canvas.

Taking Precautions

If your document or photograph is of great value, photocopy the item onto acid-free paper and frame this instead. Or, scan the item into your computer and print on acid-free paper or photo canvas material for a long-lasting effect that also allows you to "touch up" the image. This method also allows you to add accents such as dried flowers to adorn the document without worrying about acidity or other preservation issues.

(Above) If you are concerned about damaging a treasured letter, make a color copy of it before placing it in a float frame. A clear-glass float frame allows a letter to be read on the front and back.

(Opposite) A room appointed with antiques embraces a series of old documents, photographs and drawings.

CHAPTER 8

Framing Precious Memories

Author Becky Aligada wrote: "Memories are the treasures that we keep locked deep within the storehouse of our souls, to keep our hearts warm when we are lonely."

Discard our fondest memories and we would lose a precious source of great comfort. This is perhaps why the happiest of homes are filled with storytelling photographs that span an entire lifetime—or two. Images of parents, grandparents, children, husbands, wives, children and closest friends adorn our walls and line our shelves and tables because we want to remember a trip, a wedding, a birth— even an everyday occasion such as a dinner party or backyard barbecue.

Children are prolific artists in their early years. What better way to preserve special memories than in a pretty frame?

(Opposite) Priceless art comes in all shapes and sizes. Here, children's artwork gets the fine art treatment and makes them feel pretty special too.

(Right) Who says the work of famous artists has to be published? The colors of your child's artwork can be just as bold and beautiful as any prints that adorn your walls.

Young Masters

Framing your children's artwork not only personalizes your wall space, it lets your little ones know their pictures are truly a work of art. Here are some things to remember:

Use archival framing materials. Children's art is often created with materials that are not designed for longevity (e.g. newsprint, tempera paints, etc.). UV glass and preservation mat board will minimize external sources of damage, and extend the life of the artwork.

Keep the frame simple. If you plan to hang the artwork in a young child's room, keep the framing simple, vivid and bright. Children respond more readily to intense and primary colors.

Don't forget a mat. A common approach to framing children's artwork is to use a white mat along with an inner mat and a frame that matches or complements a color in the artwork.

Customize the artwork. Children's art is often dimensional, incorporating objects in a mixed-media approach. These can easily be framed using shadow box techniques, spacers, or raised matting.

Consider an acrylic box. These frames make a great "refrigerator gallery" replacement. You can even have a mat cut for the size of your little artist's favorite paper pad to help facilitate the frame change.

Children at Play

When children are young, their artwork takes center stage. As they grow, their school pictures begin to fill our spaces, and soon we're running out of frames—and space—to display it all. Almost daily, it seems, they are churning out pages of self-expression in finger paints, crayons and pencil drawings. We'd keep it all—if only we had the room.

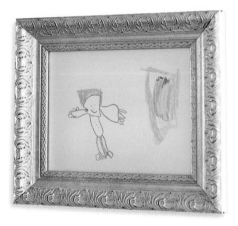

(Opposite and above) The drawings and paintings of young budding artists can lend sophistication to a room when you choose an ornate frame selection.

Family Trees

While we could say that we frame one in every hundred photos snapped, we have the room for more artwork than we think, provided we have the imagination.

Fortunately, photographs and other artwork are not relegated to a particular room, or must be displayed in one certain arrangement. The beauty in artful displays is mixing and matching frames and borrowing that concept to introduce other items into the mix. For example, a kindergartener's sketch, framed and matted, looks right at home in an arrangement of family photos with similar frames. In fact, an entire wall can pay tribute to a child's imagination and at the same time, make your little one feel pretty special.

With the proliferation in framing ideas, innovative approaches to displaying photos are all around us.

And family trees, once a diminutive element, are branching out to include dozens more photos and are available in all sizes.

Framing the Family

If you're getting ready to arrange family photographs, consider the following:

- With any framed arrangement, it is not necessary to frame each item identically. However, it does help to have some unifying element or elements to the framing designs, such as the same mats, frame finish or frame profile.

- When arranging a grouping of portraits, be sure any profile or partial profile shots are facing the interior of the grouping. Otherwise, it looks like the person in the picture is distracted or ignoring the rest of the pictures.

- An oval opening in a mat is a great option for a portrait, especially a vintage photograph. This shape is less suited for group photos since it tends to "crowd" the heads of the people at the sides of the group.

- A multiple-opening mat is an attractive way to group a number of smaller photos into a single frame. In general, it's best that the subjects in your photos are facing each other. For example, if you have two photographs side by side, the image on the right should be facing left, and in turn, the object on the left should be facing or leaning right.

(Above and opposite) A modern-day family tree is captured in a wall of family photographs framed in different frames with the same finishes and matting.

A Private Screening

Floor screens with openings that accommodate multiple 8"x10" photographs are a wonderful way to fill in a corner space and give different photos a clean, uniform presentation. While these screens come in a variety of wood finishes and photo size openings, they may not always suit a room's décor. The screen can be easily painted or given a faux treatment. For added interest, stencil the date of each family photograph under each opening.

(Left and above) Floor screens and table top screens allow you to display multiple photographs without having to hammer a single nail in the wall.

(Opposite) The same screen as shown on the left has been painted and antiqued white. The dates of the important events in the photographs shown were stenciled in gold beneath each picture.

Around The Bend

A wall leading up a stairway is a wonderful canvas to showcase your images. Even a curved wall, once considered a decorator's challenge, has been transformed into a wall of fame. A collection of small frames makes it easier to hang photographs along a curved wall. There is no need to match frames and mats, but stay in the same tones and textures for a cohesive look.

(Opposite) By keeping frames fairly small, a wall arrangement along a curved staircase makes an interesting step upstairs.

(Above) Remembering the past and the people who have enriched your life inspires an artful display of photographs at the bottom of a landing.

Poster Art

Do you know the secret to giving a movie poster the look of a million-dollar work of art? It's all in the framing. Regardless of the price, or the rarity of the poster, a bold presence can be achieved with little more than thumbtacks at each corner.

The standard frame size for movie posters is 27"x41", and there are frames available in this size and in 24"x36". If you have a smaller poster, you can fit just about any larger frame with an oversized mat to compensate for the space. Double the mat, add a fillet, step up the quality of glass and you have an above-standard work of art.

While you can dry mount a poster for a frameless effect, or choose an acrylic lightweight frame, if you want to turn a poster into a piece of art, you'll need to consider a substantial frame with a grander presence. You can pick up a poster on the streets of Paris, or special order a limited-edition reprint for a fraction of the cost of the original, but unless the frame reflects your affinity for the piece, your poster will be, well, just another poster.

(Opposite and above) A rather large poster print not only brings color to a wall, it lends interest and intrigue to a space. Remember to choose a simple frame so as to not compete with the print.

Post It!

When framing your poster, keep in mind the following:

- If the poster is simply decorative (not rare or valuable), have the poster dry mounted. This smoothly adheres the poster to a thick board and prevents waving and rippling under the frame.

- If the poster has large dark or black areas, use non-glare or anti-reflective glass or acrylic. Dark images increase the glare effect with glass, and reflections will be more pronounced.

- Avoid storing posters rolled, especially without a protective cardboard tube. If a rolled poster is hit or flattened, creases may ruin the poster.

- For posters that are large, posters that will hang over beds or sofas or posters that are within reach of children, consider acrylic or laminates rather than glass. This will reduce the weight of the framed piece, as well as provide shatter resistance.

- Take care when framing movie posters. Some are printed on both sides, with one side reversed so they will look better in a theater's light box display. Be sure the right side is showing.

(Right) For large posters that are within easy reach, consider acrylic rather than glass to avoid a piece that may shatter.

(Opposite) There's no denying a fan of horseracing lives here. Collector poster prints are a sophisticated, urban choice in this living room.

Needlework

Needlework takes hours of patience and the finished project is often an artwork in fibers. There is no need to relegate it to serving as a pillow on a sofa when it can be preserved in a frame and displayed on a tabletop easel or hung on a wall. Conventional needlepoint will need to be blocked, while some samplers will not require this step. You may wish to take your canvas to a professional needlework store to be blocked. Needlework may be protected under non-glare glass, or you may prefer to frame it without a protective cover. Either way be cautious to keep it out of direct sunlight that may fade natural wool and silk yarns and threads. It is important that needlework not touch the glass; this can be avoided by using a spacing mechanism available at frame stores such as spacer strips or a double mat.

(Right and opposite) Just as poster prints can bring color and intrigue to a room, so too can textiles such as needlepoint. A beloved sampler stitched by a grandmother ignites memories and tells a story.

Scans And Copies

If you have a handful of photographs and are struggling with fashioning a cohesive look, consider converting the images into black-and-white or sepia-toned photographs. You can photocopy images yourself using a good-quality copier or scanner and choosing black-and-white ink. Special photo print cartridges are available for printing photos in black and white.

To convert photos to sepia tone, consult a professional photographer or printer. These methods also give a vintage feel to modern snapshots as well as tie together old photos that may have been developed in different tones or have faded over the years..

(Above) If you are hesitant to cut a photo to fit a particular frame, consider copying it on a quality printer. Also, a recent snapshot can take on old-time charm by changing it from color to black-and-white or sepia tone.

(Opposite) Frames with a nostalgic touch echo prints from long ago.

CHAPTER 9

Framing The Unexpected

When shopping for an eye-catching piece of art, we often overlook the unique and sometimes rare treasures we've picked up or have been given. Personal taste and experience cannot be bought and hung on your wall. Your own life stories can.

You may have spent days hiking Mount Kilimanjaro, a feat of physical exertion for sure, and returned home with a bag full of exotic African mementos—a tribal knife, access pass to the Tanzania park, maybe a gift of music from the local tribesmen. You've got the makings of a work of art that speaks of blood, sweat and tears and would undoubtedly turn a plain space into a storytelling place.

Worth Framing

Unique items worth framing:

- Baby shoes, cups
- Bridal veil, gloves
- Christening gown
- Coins, stamps
- Collectible teacups, plates
- Dried flower bouquet
- Flag
- Golf club, ball
- Jewelry
- Medals
- Musical instruments
- Spoons
- Uniforms
- Vintage purse

(Left) This authentic jersey was framed using UV filtering to help eliminate fading.

(Opposite) What you find on your travels can inspire a creative and storied display.

Telling Your Story

After you consider your style and the room's overall decor, think about what objects you have that are interesting and are storytellers, and which ones would lend dimension and depth to a room.

It could be one object, or a handful of items, that becomes a piece of art unlike any other. When framing, you could opt for something as simple as an oversized acrylic box, or as elaborate as a gold leaf shadowbox frame to showcase a handful of medals of honor, or a quilt square picked up on a trip through Amish Country.

Once framed, a christening gown could adorn a wall in your child's room; a hole-in-one golf display is befitting a den or office space; and an arrangement that pays tribute to a favorite musical or play could decorate a living room. The important thing is that you dig out your special items and get them ready for the spotlight.

(Left) Antique fabric and laces are far too beautiful to stay in the drawer. Framing them is a perfect way to safely enjoy them every day.

(Opposite) A day at the beach inspired these framed prints and shadowbox. Trinkets large and small cannot only set the theme on a wall; they also can help create a tablescape.

An Occasion To Remember

Just about any celebration—from weddings to a baby's birth—leaves behind all sorts of items that mark the day. A cake topper that belonged to the groom's parents and is used once again at your wedding can be forever remembered in a frame. Here the delicate topper can remain, until it is called upon to commemorate the next generation's nuptials. Perhaps a beloved aunt hand-crocheted your daughter's first sweater—a precious gift for certain. Don't limit yourself— a baby's receiving blanket or favorite toy can make sentimental works of art too.

Sewn Together

Attaching your treasures to a frame backing with thread is a safe alternative to glue.

- Discreetly sewing your item to the surface of the frame's backing material is just as important as the thread you choose.
- Use thread that is most like your item: silk thread for silk items, cotton for cotton items, etc.
- For non-textile objects, such as golf clubs or a silver baby cup, loop cotton-covered polyester—it's strong enough to hold but soft enough to preserve—around the item.
- When you need lots of strength, use button thread.
- Monofilament line, or fishing line, is not recommended. It stretches over time and can damage delicate textiles.

(Right) A bouquet of hand-picked flowers was carefully pressed beneath the glass of this frame.

(Opposite) Wedding bells are ringing all year round! The elegant invite, cake-cutting utensils and other items from a fairy-tale wedding beautifully unite for a tribute beyond dreams. Above hangs the wedding cake topper. By not using glass, the frame easily accommodates the vintage topper.

Textiles And Vintage Clothing

Combining textures and textiles brings great interest to a room. Taste is undoubtedly the most important factor, and the items you choose to display, along with your choice of framing materials and methods, should reflect the distinct theme of a particular room and your own style. For example, an Egyptian scroll would be out of place in a country bedroom, whereas a piece of exotic art would look right at home in an earthy room with generous amounts of plants, natural fabrics and materials such as stone and leather.

When framed correctly, you not only ensure the preservation of a textile or piece of fabric, you make a dramatic personal statement. When framing textiles, you'll want to sew the items to the backing of the frame. In addition to textiles such as jerseys, christening gowns, baby booties and silk embroideries, many other items have sections that can be looped around with thread, such as the tips of a silk fan or writing utensils. Use an upholstery needle to stitch items, and be sure to drive a pilot hole in the backing to secure your stitching. The type of thread you use and the correct glazing material (typically a UV-protective acrylic for a large item) also is important.

Framing Textiles

Some things to remember when framing textiles:

- Frame textiles with a spacing mechanism behind glass. The spacing is necessary to keep any moisture that forms on the inside surface of the glass from wicking into the item.

- Do not alter your textile. Cutting your item to fit a smaller frame will forever ruin the piece of original art.

- Preserve your textile by framing it behind glass. This way, you will keep dust away from your textile and protect it from ultraviolet light.

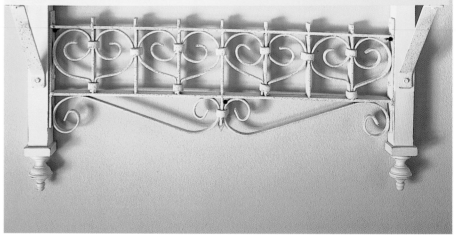

For The Love Of The Game

There's no price you can put on witnessing the dramatic conclusion to the seventh game of the World Series, especially if you caught the winning home run ball. Your treasured take-home gift may not make it into the Hall of Fame, but the ball, along with the game's entry ticket and program, have the makings of an arrangement that would make a true sports fan green with envy. Any game—be it baseball, hockey, golf, football, or soccer—can inspire a framed masterpiece with a favorite player's jersey, baseball bat or signed collectible card as the main attraction. A sports-themed hanging would make a great piece of art in a game room or a little boy's room.

(Above and right) Perfect for a boy's room or sports memorabilia-themed space, these shadowboxes capture the excitement of a home run or a hole in one.

(Opposite) Diminutive dresses and baby's bonnets make interesting pieces to frame.

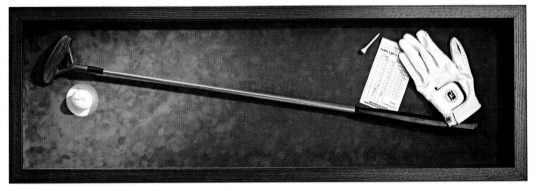

Unique Heirlooms

There are no hard and fast rules about what can be framed. If something is precious to you, it can probably be framed. China plates and teacups are no exception. If a cup and saucer is a family treasure, an excellent way to preserve it for future generations is to have it framed in a multi-dimensional frame and protected behind glass.

While a vintage record may not be of value to a collector, it may be the sound score for your all-time favorite movie. Pieces that you want to frame do not always have to be family heirlooms. They can be treasures found at flea markets, souvenirs from a recent trip, or just those items that have a personal meaning to you. For example, if you want to be "Queen for a Day" a collection of crowns is worth putting in a frame. You can design your frames so they open. If your crowns are pins or necklaces they can be removed, worn, and returned. Whatever the reason for sharing, you can't go wrong with a good frame to display your favorite things.

(Above) A treasured teacup can be reserved in a custom frame in which the saucer is adhered to a cornice moulding.

(Opposite) Albums and their covers inspire a framed piece for any music lover. Here, "The Sound of Music" is remembered through the album and its cover and pages from the program from a musical performance.

Dimensional Frame

If the item you are planning to frame is deeper than the frame, consider removing the glass and mounting the item inside the frame for a three-dimensional effect. Do remember, however, displaying artwork, collectibles and other items behind glass is the best way to protect and preserve your valuables.

Quick Change

If you prefer a background other than the one provided in a ready-made shadowbox, simply cover the existing material along with your material of choice with hook-and-loop tape for an instant redo. That way, you can change the piece as you change your décor.

(Above) A collection of whimsical items are displayed in a unique frame.

(Opposite) Travel far without leaving your room, or send yourself off to dream of faraway places, with a shadowbox filled with travel-themed items.

ANNIVERSARY DINNER

Zucchini-Watercress Soup

Fruit-Stuffed Cornish Hens
Ginger Candied Carrots
Nutted Wild Rice

Pavlova

Catherine Risling

Everett Bertino

CHAPTER 10

Special Occasions

Just like a good piece of furniture, quality frames can outlive us all. Their distinct quality of longevity leads us to craft a multitude of uses out of frames—to capture everyday sentiments and to celebrate special occasions. When selecting your frames for such celebrations you can choose to be consistent in your selection. Each frame for each guest can be the same or you can be more creative and have each frame different to suit each guest's personality. Change the frames by color; the men can be given brown enameled frames while the women are given white enameled frames. You can select your frame by the finish, with the men receiving leather frames and the women being given fabric-covered frames. Or choose by fancy embellishments, which, of course, would be diamonds for women and black onyx for men.

Remember, quality frames can always be painted, gilded, distressed or faux finished to completely change their look.

(Opposite and right) Frames can be used and reused to display a dinner party menu. Small frames make perfect place card holders.

(Above) Simple items like decorative handmade papers, nostalgic cards and antique hardware are enough to transform a frame into a lovely tray.

(Opposite) An ornate frame becomes an elegant decorative tray with complementary handles and simple knobs as feet. The glass protects what you choose to display underneath.

Tray Chic

A frame can be transformed into an elegant tray with small decorative knobs and other hardware serving as feet and handles and makes a great gift for birthdays and anniversaries. The glass provides a sturdy place to set things and makes cleaning up spills a cinch. Trays can be themed to honor a loved one, memorialize a wedding or to simply display a collection of vintage photographs, postcards or greeting cards. The background can be chosen to match the colors in a particular room, or a distinct décor. For example, handmade papers with wonderful textures are befitting an Asian-inspired room, while raw silk is a sophisticated choice for a traditional room. Rather than glass, a framed mirror can become a tray as well.

Take Your Seat

Invite your wedding guests to be seated at their table by displaying their place cards in a chic frame. Carefully remove the glass from the frame and cover the backing with batting, then a piece of fabric about two inches larger than the backing on all sides. Simply fold the material back and use a glue gun to adhere it to the backing. Strips of coordinating ribbon glued only at their bottom edge will keep the place cards in place. Once the honeymoon is over, the frame can be reused and re-hung in the newlyweds' home.

(Above) Wedding memorabilia just beckons to be showcased and preserved.

(Opposite) A large museum-style frame elegantly holds place cards at a wedding reception.

The Main Event

Special occasions worth capturing:

- Births
- Ceremonies (Bar Mitzvahs, Confirmations, scouting and other club ceremonies, etc.)
- Concerts & entertainment events
- Family vacations
- Funeral/memorial items
- Graduations
- Hobby events (prizes, contests, awards and achievements)
- Holidays (Valentine's Day, Mother's and Father's Day, Christmas, New Year's)
- Prom, Homecoming, and other formal dances and school events
- School plays or musical performances
- Sporting events
- Weddings

Reason To Celebrate

Special events such as graduations and weddings aren't just big days for the honoree. They are usual prime photo opportunities for family members together, and is all the more reason to create a photo grouping to commemorate a special day. You might consider gathering photos of other family members celebrating the same achievement or event. Groupings of couples from several generations on their wedding day is always a heartwarming display.

(Opposite) If you can't decide which photographs to frame and hang on your walls, simply sort through your stacks of snapshots and choose the ones with lots of smiles—and the ones that make you smile.

(Below) A graduation inspires this wall shelf display.

Hung With Cheer

Miniature frames also can double as memorable tree ornaments when hung from a beautiful ribbon. Remember past Christmases by adding to your frame ornaments every year. A treasured picture of smiling faces is certainly worth a thousand words that speak of happy times.

Your computer is a great tool for adjusting the size and format of favorite photos to fit into miniature frames. Use the custom size feature on your photo software and choose the size that fits the frame. For small frames, this is generally 2"x3". For a cohesive look, print all the photos in black and white.

(Above) Small frames intertwined into garland add a delightful alternative to classic holiday ornaments.

(Right) Mini-frames may also be inserted into a colorful wreath to make a cherished decoration for the wall or door.

CHAPTER 11

Custom Framing

Not every snapshot or giveaway poster requires a custom frame with a custom frame price. The made-to-order approach to picture framing has two goals in mind: preservation and presentation. If your artwork is worth a million dollars, without a doubt you should use the best materials possible to protect the piece and ensure longevity. If you simply want to make your artwork *look* like a million dollars, well then, a custom job will do that, too.

Preservation framing, also known as conservation or museum-quality framing, employs materials and techniques that help protect against the effects of sunlight and pollutants and other sources of damage that yellow, fade and destroy the art. Working with a professional framer not only promises a striking presentation that perfectly enhances the artwork, it also helps you achieve quality results and a framed piece of art destined to last a lifetime.

Beware!

Avoid hanging valuable artwork:

- Near active fireplaces
- In kitchens
- Near doors that get slammed a lot (front doors, particularly)
- Next to heat registers
- In direct sunlight

(Opposite) An elaborate frame, a sophisticated choice for this formal dining room, gives a work of art the honor it deserves.

Matting

For every framing material that is sold off the shelf, there is a preservation-minded alternative. Archival matting is acid-free and lignin-free and typically made from alpha cellulose or all-rag fiber. Improper matting can cause paper to become brittle and darken, and with some poor quality boards, the core of the board darkens with age. "Acid burn" is also common, in which the window opening becomes stained onto your photo or print. It is important to remember to use preservation-minded materials for both the mat board and the backing.

Frame Moulding

While the quality of ready-made frames is akin to custom frames, there's no comparing the diverse selection. Custom frames can be metal or wood and come in a variety of stains, glazes, paints and finishes.

Filler Boards

Filler boards are placed behind the backing in the frame to hold the contents in place without bowing when displayed. Typically corrugated, honeycombed or foam boards must be chemically inert.

(Above) When choosing a custom mat, be sure to pick a color in the painting to match.

(Opposite) Artwork is often odd-sized and requires custom frames, which makes an interesting display.

Glazing

Whether you choose acrylic or glass, you need to first consider the size of your artwork and the room in which you plan to hang it. These protective sheets, also referred to as glazing, protect the surface of the work and keep out dust and dirt. Glass is least expensive, and often easier to clean and more resistant to scratches, however, it is much heavier than its alternatives and may shatter if struck. Acrylic, on the other hand, is a lightweight alternative that is resistant to shattering. Acrylic also attracts dust and may require a special cleaner. Whichever you decide, be sure the item being framed does not touch the glass; use a thick mat board or spacers to prevent this.

Mounting

While dry mounting is recommended for low-value artwork, the preferred alternative for original, important or valuable items is hinging, or museum mounting, in which the artwork is attached with paper hinges to the board. The art hangs free, allowing it to expand or contract with humidity. Hinging, unlike the mounting process, is not permanent and therefore will not affect the resale value of the artwork. Artwork, especially paper, should be hinged to its support with Japanese rice paper and a wheat or rice starch paste. Hinging is like taping, only the acid-free materials used in the process avert damage to the artwork. Everyday tapes are harmful and should always be avoided. Archival corner pockets are another viable alternative.

Types of Glass

Anti-reflective: Features a special coating that improves the transmission of light to reduce glare without causing distortion. Similar to the high-tech coatings found on eyeglasses and computer monitors.

Acrylic (or plexiglas): A lightweight alternative to glass recommended for very large pieces, children's rooms and valuable artwork as it is shatter-resistant. Ideal for shadowboxes, artwork without mats or when using glass spacers.

Clear (regular): Used when glare is not a concern. Most affordable glass type.

Low-iron: Glass manufactured with a reduced iron content. This reduces the slight greenish cast common to most types of glass, and allows the colors of the artwork to appear more vivid and true.

UV filtering: Protection from the irreversible effects of UV damage. Protects from both natural and artificial UV light.

UV filtering and non-glare: Combines UV protection with a matte finish for glare-free viewing and enduring enjoyment.

UV filtering and abrasion resistant: Protects art from UV light while it protects itself from scratches and the abrasive effects of chemical cleaners. It can be cleaned with common household cleaners.

(Above) When having precious items such as baby photos and shoes framed, consider the heirloom quality of the pieces and choose timeless frame styles.

(Opposite) These vintage flash cards were framed using non-glare glass with UV filtering to protect them from fading over time.

Dust Cover

Every piece of custom framed art should be sealed at the back of the frame with paper. This material, called a dust cover, may be made from chemically stable paper or spun polyester film and is typically adhered completely on all four sides.

Before you begin, be sure that your valuable fabric and garments are stable. The items should be clean since soil and skin oils from handling can cause damage over time. The method of attachment should be reversible and provide adequate support so that there is an equal distribution of weight to prevent tearing or stretching.

Preserving a Lifetime

When preserving historic papers, photographs and written records, here are some things to keep in mind:

- Do not use adhesive tape. Tape has chemicals that can destroy documents.

- Do not do anything to a document or photograph that cannot be undone. This includes writing on the document or photograph in ink, having it laminated or repairing it with tape or glue.

- Keep papers in a dry, cool acid-free environment. Extreme temperature and humidity changes cause deterioration.

- Do not store papers in attics or basements. These are places where heat and humidity can do much damage.

- Keep documents out of the light. Store in metal boxes or file cabinets. For greater protection, use acid-free folders and boxes.

- Store papers flat and unfolded. After many years, it may not be possible to unfold papers without destroying them.

- Metal paper clips, rubber bands and most tape can rust or chemically destroy paper fibers. Plastic paper clips are preferred.

- Keep documents away from food and beverages, which can attract insects.

- Do not store diplomas or certificates in the folders they are presented in. The ribbons that hold the certificate in place often leave stains.

(Left) Be sure to choose the frame and mounting that will preserve and protect the fibers and textiles and that they are properly mounted.

(Opposite) A child's kimono reflects the Asian-inspired theme of this living room. Acrylic is a wise choice for a large piece.

129

(Above and opposite) Consider the moisture factor when choosing prints for a room such as a bathroom. If you custom frame your prints, be sure to inform your framer where the artwork will hang.

Moisture Control

Sealing a framed item completely off from moisture is a difficult issue. If you are framing valuable items to be displayed in an area without a stable climate, protecting the item requires the use of a heat-activated adhesive to adhere a polyester and aluminum laminated sheet to the front edges of the glass, wrapping it around the side and covering the back. Sometimes, a desiccant or conditioning material will be included to help maintain a stable and low moisture level. Since humidity is relative to temperature, even sealing the item completely does not guarantee that fluctuations in temperature will not cause problems. It is also a fairly expensive solution.

In everyday usage, it's best to slow the rate of change in moisture content within the frame to minimize condensation, rather than try to prevent it altogether. This can be accomplished with ample filler boards in the back of the frame, which help to buffer this sort of change; the standard dust cover; and the use of bumpons, or self-adhesive plastic buffers, to ensure air circulation behind the frame. If the back of the frame is in direct contact with the wall, it can allow condensed moisture from the wall into the framing package. A little air space behind the frame may help prevent this.

If you notice condensation or buckling of the matting despite these measures, consider a non-traditional framing approach, like mounting and laminating a print to a rigid backing with edges that are beveled and finished in a particular color. Although it does not allow the use of matting, it is a "sealed" solution that is safe for hanging in very humid environments, such as a bath or laundry room.

Lighting Tricks

You may have a Picasso beautifully framed and hung over your fireplace, but unless you can see it, who cares? Lighting sets the mood, illuminates your path and when it comes to artwork, directs the spotlight on the most important finishing touch in the room.

Accent lighting (also referred to as focus or spot lighting) such as track lighting, uplighting or recessed down lighting provides a dramatic focal point when aimed at artwork. When lighting your framed image, be sure that the light is just bright enough to allow the appreciation of the art since any light can damage art over time.

Recessed lighting requires cutting into the ceiling or wall, whereas track lighting, a more contemporary alternative, is mounted to the surface. Up lighting is floor fixtures that direct light upwards.

There are also picture lights, which attach directly above or below a frame and are portable and easy to install. A rule of thumb is that picture lights should be about 1/3 the width of the picture.

Glare may be a factor so to reduce its impact and to give an even distribution of light, use an adjustable spotlight that is pointed at the likeliest focal point of light in the painting.

(Above and opposite) Accent lighting can transform artwork into a museum piece. There are many options available, including this prewired strip with small spotlights.

Spotlights and picture lights, however, should be far enough away and not too bright so that they do not raise the temperature of the art they illuminate. For example, although halogen lighting provides a bright illumination with a good color spectrum, an intense, nearby halogen light can significantly heat up the art, causing it to dry out and accelerating any natural breakdown of its materials.

Be sure to experiment with different light bulbs to see which one best accentuates the colors and textures of your framed piece. Halogen bulbs, for example, are a pure white light and best simulate natural sunlight, while incandescent bulbs are yellow and warmer in tone.

133

Hanging Artwork

How you frame and where you hang your artwork will directly affect its presentation and its longevity. If you are hanging a series of photos or items, you need to determine the balanced composition, centerline, horizontal line, eye level and overall visual balance.

It is best if your horizontal line is at eye level. If you're hanging the artwork in a living room, family room, dining room or bedroom, where most people would be sitting down, you may want to consider making your horizontal center line about two feet lower than standing eye level. Eye level would best be considered the eye level averaged between the tallest and shortest person in your home.

(Opposite) Placement of frames requires thought and planning. Before a nail goes into the wall, remember to start at eye level and center your pieces above furniture and within the space of a wall.

(Right) Using an artist's approach to hanging frames—such as hanging these frames on the diagonal—gives a creative flair to custom frames.

Collages

There are a variety of ways to group your artwork. You can line them all in a horizontal line, spaced evenly; group like frames side by side to fill in a particular space; hang them so that the tops or all bottoms of the frames line up; or, if the frames are different sizes, line up the horizontal centerline of each picture in the row. With a grouping of mismatched frames, create order and balance by aligning the bottom edges of some frames with the top edges of others; aligning some left-handed edges; and centering some frames over others. Start in the center at eye level with the largest piece and build around it. Be sure, however, the entire grouping is centered.

Photo Ledges

Overlapping photo frames on a hanging ledge lends a casual look and doesn't require additional holes in the wall. Remember to vary the heights of the objects on the ledge. Attach the ledge with nails or picture hooks.

Large Artwork

There are special D-ring hangers available for large, heavy pieces of artwork that come in various sizes, depending on the piece's weight. Do not use hanging wire if the piece is extremely heavy.

Wood Frames

Most wood frames are secured with small metal points at the back, which are bent to remove the cardboard backing so that your print or poster can be inserted. A point driver makes installing the points very quick and easy.

Hanging Tips

- Before you hammer a nail into the wall, be sure you have all the artwork pulled together and you have a general idea of how and where it will be hung.

- Always hang one picture at a time to avoid nailing too many holes in your wall.

- Hanging height is generally at eye level for the room, or approximately 60 inches from the floor.

- Keep proportion in mind. For example, a 36"x48" framed picture above a side table would look out of place, and a 16"x20" framed picture would be visually dwarfed if hung alone above an overstuffed couch.

- Artwork hung above a piece of furniture should be about 2/3 the width of the furniture, and hung approximately 5 to 10 inches above the furniture.

- Hang pictures so that they form at least one horizontal and one vertical line (except in the case of a round grouping).

- Don't space out your frames too much; the width of your hand is a good amount of space.

- Never use a cleaning agent with an ammonia base on glass. The cleaners will streak and can create gassing within the frame that can damage the artwork. When it comes to cleaning acrylic, do not use glass cleaners and paper towels but rather a soft, damp cotton cloth and a special glass cleaner for plastic. Always spray the cleaner onto the cleaning cloth, not the glass. Cleaner sprayed directly on the glass can seep under the lip of the frame and soak into the matting and artwork.

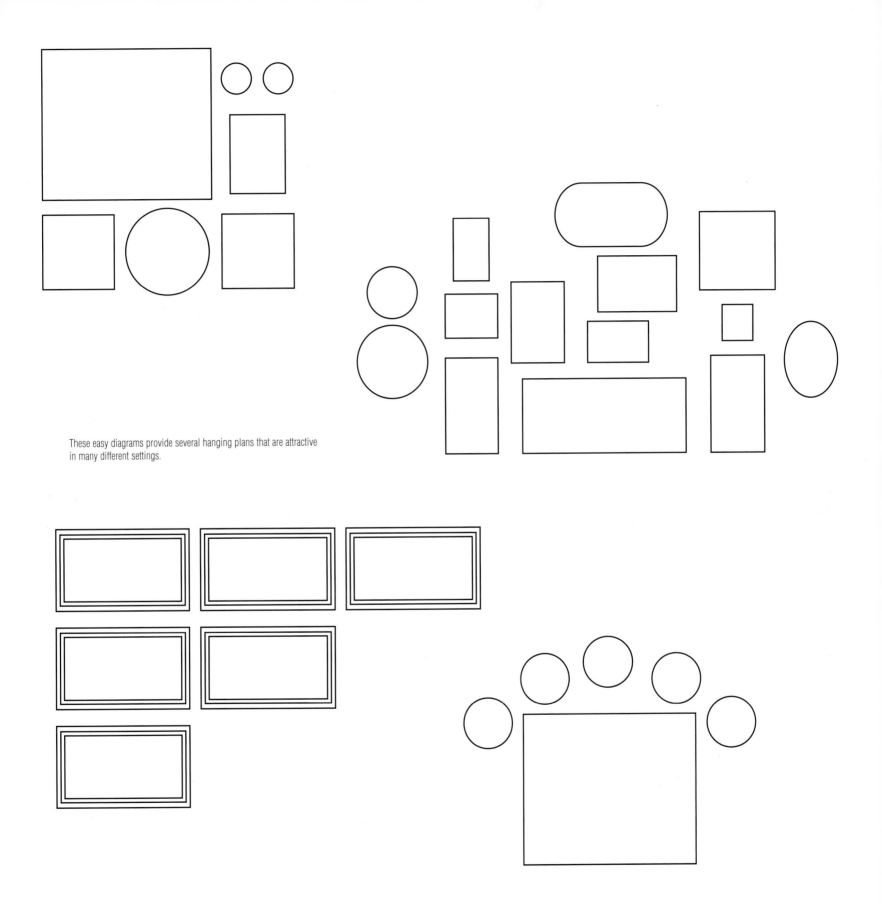

These easy diagrams provide several hanging plans that are attractive in many different settings.

Tools Of The Trade

What you'll need:

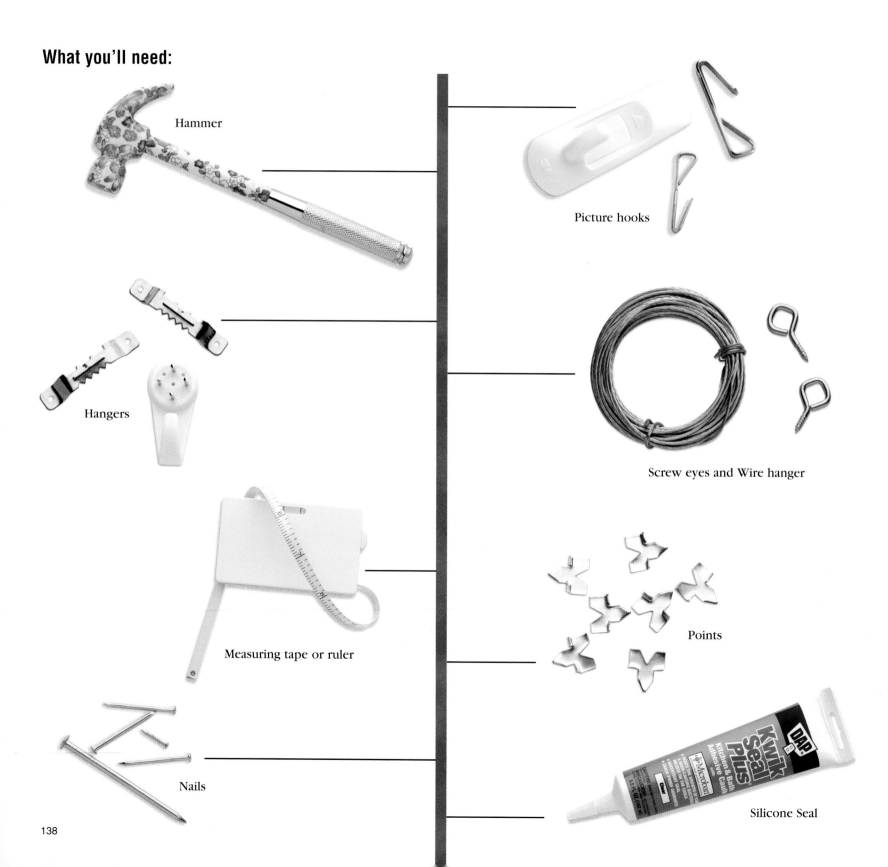

Hammer

Picture hooks

Hangers

Screw eyes and Wire hanger

Measuring tape or ruler

Points

Nails

Silicone Seal

Hanging Methods

Adhesive Hangers: A small hook attached to an adhesive strip. Does not require making a hole in the wall, but only suitable for very small, lightweight items.

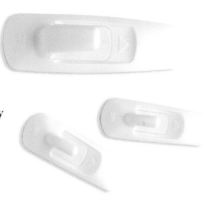

Masonry Hangers: Used for concrete and brick.

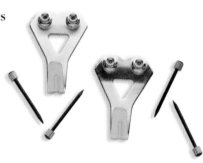

One-Piece Hangers: These consist of a nail set at an angle through a metal disk. The disk helps support the nail against the wall. The best hanger for use with sawtooth hangers on the picture as it does not extend above the hanger.

Earthquake Hangers: Attaches the picture to the wall so it will not shake off in an earthquake.

Picture Hooks: Two-piece hangers with a bent strip of metal and a nail. The metal strip provides a hook for the wire and guides the nail into the wall at an angle, providing support. These are more effective than a single nail since they help prevent the nail from tearing out of the wall. Commonly available for pictures from 5 to 100 pounds that are equipped with a wire hanger on the back.

Wall Anchors: Typically a plastic sleeve that holds a screw. A hole is pre-drilled in the wall, and the wall anchor is pounded into the hole with a hammer. When the screw is driven into the anchor, the anchor expands and provides a very secure mounting point. Wall anchors should be used for very heavy pieces, unless the hangers can be positioned over wall studs.

Sawtooth Hangers: Horizontal metal hangers with jagged edges used for smaller pieces.

Wire Hanger: Used on medium-weight artwork. Wire is loosely attached to two eye screws positioned about 1/3 down on each side of the frame.

Framing Glossary

Acid burn: Yellowish-brown lines that appear on artwork as a result of prolonged contact with acidic cardboard, mat boards or other materials.

Acid free: A term used to describe adhesives, papers, mat boards and other framing supplies that have no acid in them. Materials are more stable and less likely to damage or discolor artwork.

Acrylic: Clear plastic sheeting used in place of glass to glaze a picture. Also used to make boxes to hold large pieces and three-dimensional objects.

Archival: Framing procedure in which all materials are completely acid free and allows the item or items to be unharmed and easily removed, if desired.

Backing board: Material used behind the artwork, usually scrap mat board or foam core board. The artwork is hinged or mounted to this board.

Beveled edge: A 45-degree cut at the inside edge of a mat board window. Exposes about 1/16" of the mat board core.

Blocking: The straightening and shaping of a piece of fabric or needle art. The material is dampened, stretched slightly to straighten then tacked to a board.

Brad: A small nail used in joining frames and securing the backing board into the frame.

Conservation framing: See Preservation framing.

Conservation mounting: See Preservation mounting.

Double mat: Two separate mat boards, one on top of the other, that frame the artwork. The amount visible of the bottom mat is determined by the opening of the top mat.

Dry mount: Process of using dry adhesive tissues to mount paper artwork or photographs to a board using high heat and a dry mount press.

Dust cover: Protective sheet of paper placed on the back of wood frames to protect artwork from dust and dirt. Usually made with kraft paper and attached with special tape or glue.

Filler board: Material used behind the backing board to fill excess space in the frame. Usually foam board or corrugated board. Held in place with points or brads.

Fillet: Decorative woodstrip used as an accent inside another moulding or liner. Sometimes used under the glazing at the edge of the mat window opening.

Floating artwork: Matting technique in which mat board does not overlap the artwork, but rather, the artwork is adhered directly onto the mat board with its edges exposed.

Foam core: Stiff, lightweight material used as a mounting board. Foam makes up the center of the board with a layer of paper on each side. Used as a mounting board, backing board and as a spacer in deep frames or shadow boxes.

French mat: A mat with inked lines spaced at various intervals around a window opening. Watercolor wash often used between the lines to create a decorative panel.

Gilding: Process of applying gold leaf and/or burnishing powders to a wood frame.

Glazing: Refers to variety of glass and acrylic products used to finish and protect framed artwork. Includes conservation/preservation glass and acrylic, anti-reflective and non-glare glass.

Hinges: Strips of tape or other materials used to mount artwork in conservation framing. Typically, strips of Japanese or mulberry paper are torn and attached to the acid-free mount with starch glue.

Lacing: Conservation method for mounting textile art. Artwork is centered on a mounting board, with the excess fabric wrapped to the back of the board. With a needle, the appropriate thread is drawn through the corner of the fabric on one side and across to the opposite. This continues until the work is held firmly in place.

Laminate: A film, often vinyl, that is adhered to the surface of a poster or photograph to provide a protective and sometimes textured coating.

Lignin: A component of wood that is sometimes found in non-archival papers and boards. Lignin yellows and becomes acidic over time. Preservation-grade boards must be lignin-free as well as acid-free.

Linen tape: Tape containing a linen surface with an adhesive backing that is often used in hinging artwork.

Liner: A moulding, usually fabric covered, used inside the outer moulding in a frame. Often used in place of mats on framed oil paintings.

Lip: The thin, projecting edge of the moulding just above the rabbet; mats and glazing typically fit under the moulding lip.

Mat board: Colored paper or rag board used over artwork to create a transition from the picture to the frame and separate the art from the glass.

Mat board core: The center area of the mat board.

Mat board exposure: The reveal of the bottom mat board when one mat window is stacked on top of another. Typically ¼". Also referred to as offset.

Moulding: The material used to build a frame. Typically wood, metal or plastic.

Mounting: Methods include dry mounting, wet mounting, spray mounting, vacuum mounting, lacing, stretching, stapling and hinging.

Mounting board: Backing material used to support the artwork.

Museum mounting: See preservation mounting.

Offset: See mat board exposure.

Plexiglas: Common term for acrylic. Used in place of glass and is distortion-free, lightweight and shatter-resistant.

Preservation framing: Framing procedure where all materials that come in contact with the artwork are completely acid free and reversible. Designed to minimize the deterioration of the artwork caused by exposure to the environment by hinging artwork instead of mounting it; using high-quality acid-free mats and boards; glazing with conservation glass or acrylic. Also referred to as conservation framing.

Preservation mounting: Attaching the artwork to a preservation-grade backing board such as rag board, rice or wheat paste and mulberry hinges or other non-deteriorating materials and processes. Also referred to as museum mounting and conservation mounting.

Rabbet: The groove under the lip of the moulding that allows space for the mat, glass, art and mounting board.

Rag board: Board manufactured from cotton or other fibers. Used in preservation framing.

Spacer: Often made from plastic, foam core or mat board, it creates an air space between the glazing and the picture.

Vacuum mounting: Cold mounting system using the pressure of a vacuum press to mount paper art and fabrics to a mounting board. Either sprays or wet adhesives such as paste can be used.

Window: The opening in a mat board to view the picture underneath.

Acknowlegments

Aaron Brothers
www.aaronbrothers.com

Written by Catherine Yarnovich Risling
Photo Styling by Rebecca Ittner

Aaron Brothers

Kathryn Henkens
Vice President/General Merchandising Manager

Katrina George
Assistant Buyer/Design Specialist

Marguerite Hill
Corporate Attorney

Paul Jones
Associate Buyer

Donna Kleinman
Senior Buyer, Wall, Photo Frames

Sven Olsen
Buyer Custom Framing

George Rodriguez
Assistant Buyer, Custom Framing

Leticia Rohrbach
Public Relations/Advertising

Lights Now
www.lightsnow.com

Photography by:
Ryne Hazen
Chris Little
Mark Tanner
Jessie Walker
Scott Zimmerman

Special thanks to Interiors by Decorating Den,
Christy Repassy, Susan Rios, and Michael and
Chris Somogyi.

The following photographs reprinted by
permission of Hearst Communications, Inc.

M. Skot ©1994   3
Susan Gentry McWhinney ©2002   21
Jim Hedrich   23
William P. Steele ©1994   48, 98

Index